POST MY QUOTES ON SOMETHING

JERVON SALTERS

I0151249

Marco Media Marketing Management
9950 US HWY 521 STE D
Greeleyville, SC 29590

Why I Wrote This Book

If the legacy I want is never fulfilled, then I can say I never went a day without trying to make it happen. It is all about maximizing yourself as a person and using all the tools you have to beat the odds. I want my wife to be proud that my big dreams that she patiently waited on came to light. I want my sons to know that daddy tried a little bit of everything so that he could tell them and prepare them for being a man. I want my daughter to be inspired and be wowed by her dad to seek someone similar and to always be a woman first. My mother gave me all she could and showed me what a GIANT HEART can do. She taught me to give, help, inspire and make others smile. To my brothers and my sisters, this is a cold world designed to bring down the best and we are too strong for that. Together, like a rope, hold on and we will survive it all. To my father whom I miss, the strongest and most silent teacher I have ever known. All you said came to light. Thank you! To everyone else, if I never told you I got love for you, I always will. Thanks to everyone present and past from across the road, to through the woods, to across the field and through the path.

Special thanks Marie, Daniel and my other family.

Introduction

In life, we will always run into things that are challenging. Sometimes we get on social media and tell the world about our challenges. Have you ever gone on Facebook and was able to tell when a person is having a relationship or basic life problems? Usually, the same problem occurs over and over. I feel that the cure to problems should start with preventing them first. The worst battle to lose is the obvious battle with the same techniques by the same person. Let life problems become life lessons. We live in a digital world and the days of a person sitting down and having time to read seem to have dwindled away. We look at a Facebook status, a few tweets and keep it moving. I think that a good quote is like advice from a good parent. A quote can motivate you, keep you cognizant, and be a quick lesson that you can apply to your everyday life. These are original quotes that I posted daily at work to help create a positive environment and positive thinking. I found that there is value in experience and observation. So, why not share it?

Peace Jervon,
In loving memory
of my father Ciceroe Salters

Table of Contents

How to Use These Quotes

I'm a person that is big on preparation and being preventive. Most of my quotes are about consequences, life, and learning from your experiences and others.So, use these to help others, such as the friend that keeps falling victim to society, the mother trying to guide her son, the family member that needs something to hold onto, or the person that wants to send his/her loved ones something to let them know they do care. Post my Quotes on Something!

Where to Post These Quotes
On a Sticky
On Facebook
On Twitter
Get it tattooed (not on face)
On your license plate
In a Text
In an Email
In your purse
On a letter in the mail
In your mind

Quote 1

If the same punch beats you every time, then you're not the boxer, you're the punching bag.

Quote 2

Television shows you the rich but never show the hard work.The streets show you hard times,fast money and gimmicks.Growth teaches you to separate truth from entertainment.

Quote 3

A camera is a hand held artist that only can duplicate.

Quote 4

A person telling you a story
of his or her hard times
growing up is a story being
told by a survivor.If they can
tell it they made it through it.

Quote 5

It's not in a snake's job description to tell you if it's venomous or not. You have to do your homework or become a victim to that snake's venom. Life can be the same way.

Quote 6

What if Tiger Woods never
touched a golf club? He
might be like many
of the youth in the inner-city
throughout america.
Kids need options.

Quote 7

The errors of the past should be the wisdom of the future,but man's desires has a way of bullying the powers of wisdom.

Quote 8

An evil man smiles
when no-one's looking.
A slick man does evil things
when no one's looking. A
wise man acts silly when no
one's looking,but a fool does
foolish things while
everyone's looking.

Quote 9

Never ignore consequences
or take them lightly,
they follow every action.

Quote 10

Life is like a seed in the ground.If you don't nurture it, then it will remain just something unnoticed and walked on.

Quote 11

Discipline and love goes hand and hand,but don't get it confused. The World and Momma will both discipline you but only one will show you love!

Quote 12

Being a part of the problem
creates the need for
more solutions.

Quote 13

Man's most important moment is the five minutes before he falls asleep! He thinks about his true, feelings, and true situation without anyone to impress.

Quote 14

Don't expect to always be happy nor should you never accept always being unhappy.

Quote 15

If you don't help
yourself when you're
uncomfortable,Don't expect
much when you get
comfortable.

Quote 16

I was told, it's not what you know but who you know,but I was shown it's not who you know but who can vouch that they know you.

Quote 17

Sometimes you don't know you went too far, until you realize you can't turn back.

Quote 18

Allow someone or something to motivate you in a positive way,or society will leave you with no options and just drag you where it wants.

Quote 19

Procrastination is the first step to your dreams never reaching the reality stage.

Quote 20

You can live by your own rules, but rarely do you get to choose the consequence for living by your own rules.

Quote 21

Who is the next king to achieve his goal?
Every man has King attributes but only the ones that give his all will be crowned King!

Quote 22

A father that rebuilt himself
when he has been broken
is a master carpenter.
Who better to teach his
children to build themselves
than a master carpenter!

Quote 23

If you cannot keep your secrets,then don't expect others to keep them.

Quote 24

The mirror is a powerful tool you look in it and it shows you who you are. You only see what you put in front of it.

Quote 25

It is hard to get the answers you need when you have no idea of the correct questions you should be asking.

Quote 26

A man that never came in 1st place should seek what he's great at and pursue it. A lifetime of 2nd place or less don't give a person much to look forward to.

Quote 27

Everyone has greatness within them, but as humans we knowingly and unknowingly allow junk to be piled on top of it.

Quote 28

When all you know is all that destroys you,then your appetite for destruction outweighs your appetite for success.

Quote 29

The greatest gift to man
has already been given.
The mind, when used it can
be powerful,but when
neglected,it can be man's
greatest foe.

Quote 30

The world is full of puppets people being strung along by desire, comfort, and instant gratification.Pop the strings, stand up and take control.

Quote 31

Perception has a slick way
of overpowering reality.

Quote 32

Time doesn't always equal wisdom. Time is also used for ignorance to marinate.

Quote 33

Creating a light at the end of a tunnel can give a man direction and take him out of the dark.

Quote 34

The ghetto didn't ask for drugs.

Quote 35

Don't let life live you
without living it a little first.

Quote 36

Love seem to be the island that everyone would like to go to,but don't have the boat or plane to get there.

Quote 37

A person can become many things in just a few seconds a liar, a father, a killer, a winner,a hero, and etc.

Quote 38

Dependency is a tool often used to control poor people ability to fully develop.

Quote 39

Looking holy to man doesn't mean you are holy in God's eyes.

Quote 40

When momma and grandma gave up on you,then you're probably on the wrong path.

Quote 41

Some crimes should equal instant insanity.

Quote 42

When life gives you
a hundred reasons to cry,
show life you have a
thousand reasons to smile.

Quote 43

Never let your body
outgrow your mind.

Quote 44

When I got out of high school,I was told get a degree.Then I was told I need experience.Then I was told I was over qualified. Can you relate?

Quote 45

If you and I are both
complaining about gas
prices,then don't you dare
look down on me.
Our money is similar.

Quote 46

If a store can sell water
and a zoo can sell animal
waste,then don't tell me I
can't be successful!

Quote 47

The ghetto is a 40-year plan to build condos on cheaper property.

Quote 48

The day you have a child is the day you must convert the word 'I" to "Us" and the word 'Can't" to "Must".

Quote 49

My worst fear is leaving my kids too early in this cold world without me teaching them all that I can.

Quote 50

Everyone has a different common sense,so be more specific.

Quote 51

Most people die never knowing what they are really good at.

Quote 52

Nino died, Scarface died, if you watched both movies fully you notice that they both lost.Don't just pick out the highlights to idolize.

Quote 53

We often live life
in the shadows of others,
fears, lies, and dreams.

Quote 54

Throw love out the window and follow your passions. It will last longer because the word love is usually political.

Quote 55

When I started dating, an older guy advised me to never let emotions be the reason you lose your life. Yes it is her house and yes she did invite you over, but her ex-boyfriend standing outside of her front door never did let go.

Quote 56

Retirement without work is almost like a myth.

Quote 57

Your problems aren't original; It's always a song that tells your story.

Quote 58

A company that needs a diversity program most likely has suspect hiring practices and the program is a fake attempt to cover it up.

Quote 59

If everyone is doing the same thing, then think twice before you do it.

Quote 60

Don't make a habit out of ignoring consequences.

Quote 61

Men would rise to a woman's standards if he was required to.

Quote 62

People have turned church into a stage for politics.We look good, say the right things, and we promise to do right,but when we walk out the door it was all politics.You fooled no one!

Quote 63

When your confident, others can see it and sometimes get curious about how and why your confident.

Quote 64

Don't tell me to ignore your disrespectful friend because that's how he is.Being disrespected is never optional to me.

Quote 65

In a relationship your 100% ,is only 50%.

Quote 66

Sometimes the finish line is only the start of a whole new race.

Quote 67

Some people don't want to move up nor do they want you to move up and will hate you for even trying.

Quote 68

A person can go further when they can see further. A person can see further when they are exposed to greater things.

Quote 69

The man that broke your leg on purpose doesn't want to hear about your fast recovery.

Quote 70

I would rather give you fifty dollars for something that can help you ,than give you the dollar you use to bring you down.

Quote 71

The human life is like a car. It must be serviced to get the most out of it.They also differ.When the car goes down it can be replaced, and a car doesn't have regrets.Service yourself physically and mentally.

Quote 72

The road to the Good Life
can be just like the yellow
brick road in the Wizard of
Oz.You will run into the
heartless, the brainless, and
many cowards,but if you
stay on the right path,
then you will survive
the movie of life.

Quote 73

Isn't it mysterious how a child can get its hand burnt on a stove one time and learn a lesson about heat while we as adults touch the sizzling stove of life over and over and never learn a lesson?

Quote 74

Most people are diamonds in the rough, but because we have the ability to make choices,we often hold ourselves down, never leaving the rough.

Quote 75

In relationship, there is no one size fits all.Every situation is different.

Quote 76

Why fear death but not fear
the things that lead to death?

Quote 77

I don't believe in karma.
I feel the worst villain will
eventually smile just like a
clean cut person will
eventually deal with pain
and problems.

Quote 78

The world's population would be different if the requirements for bearing a child was true love.

Quote 79

Most new thoughts are only shadows of older thoughts.

Quote 80

If your life was shown at a movie theater, would you be bored? Would you yell at the screen? Would you walk out? Or would you smile? Or would you be mad at your own script?

Quote 81

Often people live the lotto life putting time, money, and energy in a game designed to take in way more than it pays out.

Quote 82

Take time to learn yourself,
your worth and your position
in this world.

Quote 83

I rather eat pork-n-beans
with my family than to send
steak from a distance.

Quote 84

Once I was like a tire, going in circles. Today I'm like the tree, moving up.

Quote 85

In the end, men usually learn that the most important things in life has more to do with inner peace than it has to do with money.

Quote 86

Some people are no slicker than a grizzly bear hiding behind a light pole but, in their mind,they got all the sense.

Quote 87

Don't be disappointed when others won't do for you won't you don't have the drive to do for yourself.

Quote 88

The old blind man you pass daily could actually be the old wise man that's watching your every move and pulling the wool over your eyes.

Quote 89

A man's pride is a clear path to his demise when he constantly choose pride over thinking.

Quote 90

Only two words end in GRY:
hungry and angry.
These are also two things
that can destroy men because
hunger easily can turn to
greed and anger can easily
turn to trouble.

Quote 91

A lie is something everyone tell at some point,but it's sad when you tell them so much that you start believing your own lies.

Quote 92

When you have been doing
wrong for so long that it
feels better than right, then it
might be time to do
what you think is wrong

Quote 93

Today I saw a man jump off his motorcycle, running full speed along the highway.I thought the man's life was in danger.Driving slowly, I looked and saw him picking up a turtle crossing the road.He then safely put it in a nearby ditch.If we all had that same energy toward seeing the next man make it, then more people would make it to the golden ditch of life.

Quote 94

Never get so caught up in chasing love that you forget to stop loving yourself first.

Quote 95

The hardest part of being an untrustworthy person is the fact that when its time for you to do the trusting you feel the world is just like you untrustworthy.

Quote 96

Greed can cloud the mind and put a dark cloud over loyalty.

Quote 97

If a person made 100,000 dollars in year 2000 and got locked up for 10 years he lost freedom and family for less than minimum wage.

Quote 98

Some lessons are best learned through watching others. Some things you only get one try, and instantly loose all control.

Quote 99

Its life,
then the song.

Quote 100

If a man is always speaking of changing his life,most likely he is doing things he need to stop, so he can change his life.

Quote 101

Always give the talents you were born with an opportunity to work for you, then your talents will work for you.

Quote 102

A man that never had a
father then makes a child
and never tries to be a father,
is like a warrior that can save
his people but would rather
take a beauty nap!

About Me

I consider myself a boy from a little dirt road. I was raised in rural Salters, South Carolina. I am the youngest of my siblings. Being that I was 12 years younger than my brother, I was often alone. I had a giant supporting cast and strong parents. I had a lot of freedom, but what good is freedom when you had a father that made you afraid to do wrong? I never had the highest grades because they didn't matter to me. My father was more into me working hard. In school I was a clown, how else could I get attention? My cousin Shawn called me dumb. My good grades started when I got in high school and I became an honor roll student. I then enrolled myself into college and I received my BA in Sociology from SC State University, then my MA in counseling, and I almost finished with my MA in Criminal Justice. I will always be a student because life has many lessons. My motto is: I want everyone to win; a taste of first place is all people need.

www.ingramcontent.com/pod-product-compliance
Lightning Source LLC
LaVergne TN
LVHW051353080426
835509LV00020BB/3414